Thief

Poems and Prose

Bianca Bowers

Other books by Bianca Bowers

Poetry
Death and Life (Paperfields Press, 2014)
Passage (Paperfields Press, 2015)
Love is a Song She Sang From a Cage (Paperfields Press, 2016)
Pressed Flowers (Paperfields Press, 2017)
Butterfly Voyage (Paperfields Press, 2018)

Fiction
Cape of Storms (Auteur Books, 2019)

THIEF
COPYRIGHT © 2023 BIANCA BOWERS
Published by Paperfields Press
Book Cover Design by Bianca Bowers
Book Cover Art © Lisima (Shutterstock ID 795263893)

All rights reserved. No part of this publication may be reproduced, distributed, or transmitted in any form or by any means, including photocopying, recording, or other electronic or mechanical methods, without the prior written permission of the publisher, except in the case of brief quotations embodied in critical reviews and certain other noncommercial uses permitted by copyright law. For permission requests, email the publisher:
"Attention: Permissions"
info@paperfieldspress.com
www.paperfieldspress.com

ISBN-13: 978-0-6484426-9-1
EPub ISBN-13: 978-0-9942404-8-4

First Edition 2023

Contents

INTRODUCTION	xi
Where have the words gone?	11
Mathematics	12
Tattooist	14
On my way to visit you	15
In the land of Chagall	19
Gold Finch	22
Tempo Rubato	24
Time	27
Karma	28
Spiteful	29
Ketamine	31
Rome	32
Russia	34
Quiet Deaths	35
Drone	37
I wanted to cure loneliness	38
Exit Wound	39
End of my life	40
Drowning	41
Oldest dream in the book	42
Vulnerable as a human	43
Eurydice	45
A dance without music	46

Billie Eilish	47
Lucid Dreaming	49
Mockingbird	50
Odin	51
Grandfather	52
Lepidopterist	53
Egypt	54
1326	55
Europa	57
Hotel	59
Freezing Point	60
Love reimagined	61
I wanted to murder loneliness	62
Ode to becoming a love letter	65
A Happy Man	67
A blossom of hope	68
Gold thread	69
Ghostwriter	70
Ripening	71
Koru	73
Egg Shells	75
Medusa	76
Love Poem	78
Peony Pavilion	80
Mudita	81
Linguist	82
Thief	84

NOTES & ACKNOWLEDGEMENTS	86
ABOUT THE AUTHOR	92
A NOTE FROM THE AUTHOR	94
OTHER BOOKS BY BIANCA BOWERS	95

Introduction

Poetry frequently warrants an element of autobiography. Broadly, it conveys a truth not produced in fiction. You may find yourself, when reading some of these pieces, with an urge to reach out to the poet, such is their evocatively traumatic content. Yet it is the heartbreak and despair of writer's block that is at the core of much of this verse.

Taking a deeper dive, the tragedy of regret is captured in poems such as 'Time' and 'Spiteful', the latter an impressively devastating piece where even what little resolution offered in the poem plays into the mood of futility. The former piece, meanwhile, seems to provide a little more hope to the poet-narrator and their reader.

It would be fair to suggest that many of these compositions have a kind of multi-level profundity, and that some of them are rewarded with a little research or outside-the-book insight. 'Rome' is paid off with a little knowledge about the Roman poetess Sulpicia, whom Bowers draws on in the piece. However, the interludes in the collection that may require a little study are few and far between; the work stands more than adeptly on its own.

While not frustratingly difficult to decipher, these poems

can also be consumed in a variety of senses – literal, figurative, and metaphorical. For instance, 'Ketamine' could be interpreted as clever interplay between the poet and a drug-addled object of affection, or perhaps a dismissal of concepts such as the unacknowledged anonymity, and the lack of recognition for talent, that plagues many an artistic temperament, or it might be a simple meditation on unrequited love. The beauty of many of these poems is that they have more than one interpretation – and, as the postmodernists have suggested in the past – reader interpretation is as significant as authorial intent.

The reader can rely on their own life experiences to plumb the psychical depths explored throughout this rich collection. There is much to examine, admire and address here, such as male-female relationships, the loss of inspiration, and insights on the quiet resolve of emotional breakdown that frequently takes place, rather than a more outward and chaotic relinquishing of control that is more often warranted at such times.

Gender dynamics are crucial to some of the work. Fellatio features in a couple of the compositions, in part to convey how one-sided this sexual transaction can be. One could argue too that there is an undercurrent of pushback from the sanctity of domestic bliss and its associated setting – it's tautologous to say that women have historically borne the brunt of home-making exertion in the Rich North, toiling with little reward, frequently contending with alcoholic husbands keen to spend all their wages in the pub. Similar scenarios continue to play out in the Poor South. Indeed, with absentee fathers and broken families, they are still all too common in the West. Some of the pieces here could be – at the very least – visceral ventures that explore rebellion against and rejection of the status quo of the nuclear family.

As with much great work of its kind, these compositions require and reward more than one reading. Ultimately, the poems are extremely satisfying on intellectual and emotional levels, many of them expressing a range of processes that include solipsism, existential despair, heartbreak, and love.

—Richard Gibney

Where have the words gone?
April 2019

From a seaside grave, windswept and littered
with dead petals, I ask
where have the words gone?

Did I leave a billabong
syllables near Cedar
creek, did I crush my mother
tongue underfoot, the crater's lip
heavy with thought

Did I pin epitaphs to baobabs
when dreaming, Africa's cradle doused
Kerosene, burning the past
in a shaman's fire

Did I forfeit the alphabet
first degree burns, a dark-haired stranger
in his eyes, tinder, in his heart
begging me, to strike a match

All over again, I can't remember
where I left off, while disturbing the universe
so carelessly

Mathematics
16 August 2019

It is August sixteenth
and I am fuller than I wish to be
Winter has crept inside me
with the stealth of a spy

I let my forty fifth birthday pass
three days ago
without so much as a wink
Like a crowd of strangers
I spurned its presence, glued my eyes to the floor

The full moon coincided with it all
I shed blood, reflecting moreover
on that inconvenient hourglass that will soon dry up
along with any superficial beauty
I might have possessed once
upon a summer ago

But as I write this pathetic account
of a woman falling
short of her adolescent expectations
the soft afternoon sun is warm in my cheerful writing room
and I hear:
my son, watching Stranger Things

my daughter, singing over Billie Eilish
my husband, haggling with Optus, and

These anxieties
that graze my knees
cripple my muscles, on occasion
are so insignificant in the grander scheme
of a boundless soul in a finite body
and I ask myself, how long

'til you live fully?
before you die, piecemeal?
When you're forty-six or fifty?
When you weigh what you did at twenty?
When you write a book that pays for a roof?

and I think to myself, perhaps
It has nothing and everything
to do with mathematics
For as long as life is a calendar,
a scale,
a calculator...
this human can never truly be happy.

Tattooist
1 May 2020

I remember poetry
a classroom
I gatecrashed

English roses
with alabaster names
—Elisabeth, Anne
Emily, Jane

placing words—
undulating, tangerine—on loose leaf
as delicately as pink fish
roe on cream sashimi

while crimson wasps swarmed
my throat and fingers, welted
More tattooist
than poet

On my way to visit you
13 November 2020

On my way to visit you, wildflowers of every hue peeked out from grassy clumps and tree stumps, wire fences and box hedges. The white stigma of the fuchsia bougainvillaea resembled eyes as I passed by—*the big brother of the plant kingdom*, I thought. The rainbow eucalyptus near the swings is shedding bark, and the channel-billed cuckoos are back from Papua New Guinea for the summer. I hear them all the time, even at night when the frogmouth calls and the stone curlews hiss and screech at the red fox that stalks the undergrowth beneath the water pipes.

Last week I saw a kookaburra swoop across a blanket of Singapore daisies and extract a juvenile carpet python with its beak. The unsuspecting reptile didn't stand a chance. Speaking of close encounters, my daughter narrowly escaped stepping on an eastern brown snake while walking alongside a billabong yesterday, and then my rescue hound, Honey, had a close call with a cane toad, nearly ingesting its deadly toxin. Cane toads are a blight on the natural environment and a threat to wildlife. Queensland sugar cane farmers introduced the toads from South America before environmental factors were in vogue. Cane toad numbers are now in the millions and impossible to control, because there are no natural predators. I've heard a rumour, though, and seen the odd sign, that there is a river rat who has adapted and learnt to kill the toad by flipping it onto its back and driving claws into its heart, cleverly avoiding the toad's toxic glands on its back. Nature is constantly fascinating!

Since I last visited, the young tulipwood trees, planted by the council, are offering shade and I'm pleased to report zero incidents of vandalism by the so-called tunnel-snake-teens. Oh, and did I tell you that a pair of ravens have chosen to build a nest in the mountain gum tree that towers over our pitched roof? I throw a chicken carcass every few days and they drag it into the secret garden and pick it bare in minutes. Knowing my reverence for those black-feathered birds, you can imagine my delight each day as I peer up into the sky and know that raven magic is literally breeding in my backyard. I expect it will usher in the change of fortune that has already begun.

For most of my 45th year, I pointedly scrunched up my dreams—such pretty pieces of paper, decorated with cursive and art, fed like expired waste to the yellow wheelie bin. That same year, I tried to remove my heart too, but its violet veins stubbornly clung to their crimson chamber. Still, I resigned myself to never love again—citing silliness and old age as perfectly valid, if not legally binding, reasons. I could blame circumstances for getting the better of me that year, but a one-sided story is no better than a bare-faced lie. Now, in my 46th year, that long desert night is miraculously tapering off. If you look close enough you will see a scattering of tiny buds breaking forth on the horizon. I am starting to blossom again.

I think of you often; I thought you might like to know. But thinking about you and seeing you is the difference between jacaranda trees before and after October. Before, their bare branches and grey trunks blend into the landscape to such an extent that they might as well be invisible. Until one morning in October, you wake up to see clusters of purple petals adorning those nondescript trees of September.

Between visits, I am a nondescript tree, but today, on my way to visit you, I am that glorious jacaranda that turns heads and induces smiles, and I dare hope that you feel the same way.

I am at the gate now, picking up a rusted Coca-Cola tin and smelling the jasmine flowers as a gush of wind rushes down the hill. Soon I will be walking up the driveway checking your citrus trees for signs of fruit. If you are in the kitchen, put the kettle on. I have in my possession an ornate tin brimming with cloudberry tea leaves; I will brew us a fresh pot.

Bianca xo

In the land of Chagall
21 January 2021

Goats bobbed on the ocean
Fish clambered over mountains
The daytime sky wore a navy blue coat—
    silver stars, bright as suns,
    glistened on its hemline

Everything was out of place, and simultaneously exactly where it should be.

My ruby red heart was planted in the body of a man who was destined to love me
The seeds of his sorrow had flourished into happy buds and my own rib cage was home to climbing yellow flowers.

He did not recognise me when I kissed his cheek
but a memory stirred and his eyes shone like the sun that should have been
    He asked me if we'd met before
    "Yes and no," I said.
    He cocked his head and drank me in with curious eyes. "How can that be?"
    "We are the dreams that float above human souls, waiting, always waiting on them to choose love over fear."

His expression cast a shadow while he thought about it. "Are you saying that we, you and I, are destined to be together?"

I nodded.

"But?"

"But our humans are like lotus roots mired in deep mud, and they cannot see what awaits them."

He inched closer and touched my cheek. "What can we do to help them?"

"We're not supposed to interfere, but my human is close to a breakthrough and it is not against the rules to nudge her."

"How can we nudge them?" he said.

"Take my hand and walk with me to the garden under the sea."

"The garden under the sea? I have not heard of this place, yet it sounds so familiar."

I picked a yellow flower from my rib cage and a pink bud from his heart. "These pink flowers were seeds of sorrow once upon a time, and these yellow flowers that bloom each morning and close each night are a reminder of the eternal sun that always rises and sets, no matter what."

"You know about my sorrow?"

I nodded. "Yes, I was there when the flower of life saved your broken heart. And I have been waiting for you to heal and return to me."

Tears pricked his eyes as realisation dawned. "You mean, you are she?"

I nodded again.

He dropped to his knees and wrapped his arms around my thighs. "You left me in the physical world, but you have been waiting for me in this spirit realm."

I placed my hands on his shoulders. "Yes."

He looked up at me. "If only I had known. I would have healed faster and found my way back to you earlier. Why did I wait so long? Why did I try to kill myself instead of heal?"

I touched his cheek. "My love, do not berate yourself. The human world is a veil and not a mirror. Life unfolds at its own pace. We cannot rush it, or compete with it, or cheat it."

He stood up and dried his eyes. I reached for his hand and our fingers intertwined.

"Come," I said. "Let us go now, to the garden under the sea, where the flower of life waits for us to pluck a petal of renewal."

We walked down the hill, hand in hand. Blue crabs scurried in and out of green blades of grass. Ravens bobbed on the waves and whales swam in the sky. My rib cage was a ball of sunshine. His heart was bursting with fuchsia flowers. Everything was out of place and simultaneously exactly where it was supposed to be.

Gold Finch
5 February 2021

A gold finch flew into my mind
during lunch
Willing to trade a ruby feather
for breadcrumbs and cheddar

And as I held that feather, I thought about birds, wild and caged:

Was poetry a caged bird with clipped wings, or was I a bird who had forgotten how to fly?

Had the gold finch always been there—
suspended in time
silent and grounded
surviving within the confines of my own head?

And with the gold finch flew the question:

*What is a poem but a moment
and what is a poet but a curator of that moment?*

Indeed, have I lost the phenomenon of moments
or have I been flying above every moment
instead of settling now and then?

Though I know the answer already
I will settle on the branch of this moment
and ponder it a little longer.

Tempo Rubato
4 April 2021

Chopin's wistful notes drift
along night's collarbone

like waylaid smoke
an exposed tune,
      in sync with the vulnerability that haunts my
fingers,
hovers

The days, nights and seasons have stretched
longer than solstice
and fallen now, like brittle leaves
Mourning is threadbare

My bird-like wrists have grown hollow
twigs without wings
the corner of my eye accumulates
doubt builds beneath
dusty keys of an Underwood

Poetry has never left before—
always incessant;
an endless, restless ocean
Churning and turning
Now, it is quiet

heavy as the dead sea
And though I try to anchor them
with dread and desperation, my fingers float
to the surface

Through billowing lace curtains, I watch
the pianist's passion
So delicate, his ferocity,
unrivalled
I permit myself to inhale
the intoxicating scent of longing
forbidden and repressed inside me
deeper than dermis,
deeper than the sea,
deeper than this haunting dream
But now, surfacing

like an anchor, untethered
it floats into view
Waiting,
for that dramatic moment when the muse and I become tangled and suspended
Tempo rubato
So that I can whisper back
with lyrical words and renewed appreciation
for this gift, called poetry
for this velvet throne, called poet
For this illusive state, called Be(e)ing

that I rejected, denied, took for granted

The pianist hunches his angular features,
pauses
Silence prickles my skin with goose bumps
Then,
an exhaustive exhale
before the exquisite music of my heart
unravels
like yarn in my hands

Time
24 April 2021 at 13:26

Time hangs on a clothesline
Snagged by a peg
it wriggles and writhes
But I don't set it free
like I would a dragonfly or a bee
I tell it to be still
I tell it to contemplate this moment of powerlessness
when it's expending every effort to progress, to succeed, to evolve, to heal—
only to be snagged by an invisible peg
And I tell it:
> *time is no friend*
> *while you flail and fail*
> *like a helpless insect in a spider's web*

And I ask time a question; I give time an ultimatum: I say, "Time, if I set you free from that peg, will you help unsnag me from my past failures and limitations?"
To which time replies: "You don't need my help. I have seen your future, and the only thing you need is to believe in yourself."

Karma
25 June 2021

Her roots were never in question
It was the life inside her head that undulated like
hooked bait in a busy river

Fuelled by karma, he never let her go
Even if it meant bottling and preserving
the surface like fruit, even if it meant
pickling the waters of his intuition

And though she tried to tell him
She knew not how to love
a figment of her heart, She knew not
how to love him below the waterline
of longing

Where she once drowned so enthusiastically
Where she once sunk like an ill-fated wreck

Spiteful
30 January 2022 at 23:37

The sky is dark tonight
Moonless in every sense

True love is a fairytale
and I am no princess with a happy ending

I have never confessed to being lonely
But I must confess that I am lonely now

There is little left from my choices
besides regret
Regret that I have wasted so much time pretending
to be happy, pretending
to agree, pretending
to be someone else, pretending

I pull a raven's feather from my mouth
I have choked on this black heart long enough
A century of deceit is not enough payback
for the life I have wasted on my own destruction
Torture
at each point of the compass

All that's left is a grave
shallow enough to rescue time, but deep

enough to bury the curse
on this life, the last life, and any future lives
that fester beneath karma's skin

When the moon is missing from its place in the sky
I am lonely,
and fate seems so spiteful

Ketamine
23 January 2022

I wonder who lives behind his smile
Is there blood in his thoughts
when choosing coffee over conversation?

I wonder if he's sedated
—a cocktail of halcion and ketamine
and if he sees me tripping

on stardust from another planet
How could he not see
me disappear

a crater of loneliness
How could he not know
love is a drug

and I am high all the fucking time

Rome
28 February 2022

within, at the edge of the world
Sulpicia fell. A seed of love,
or its doppelgänger, planted
between ribs, tendrils of longing
Belonging

beneath reflections
Cerinthus left
so many pretty flowers
inside Rome's ageing body
A colosseum no longer
crumbling,
the gladiator's legacy exhumed

Inside, she grew taller
than yesterday
Taller than the morning
Taller than the words she had spoken and kept

Like dormant cicadas, words broke forth
from their dream, from their sleep, from their dark
night of the soul
At last, they broke free,
she broke free

Because of C—
she emerged, in a garden of butterflies
Because of C—
she was no longer museum
with wanting walls; something to admire,
forget

Because of C
because of C
because of C
She plucked wild flowers from roots
and soaked petals in fragrant hope

Russia
3 March 2022 at 04:21

While Russia invaded the Ukraine, I underwent my own invasion. An invasion I didn't resist. An invasion I happily submitted to. For that invader was not an external military force advancing to conquer and colonise me. The invader was an internal part of myself that I had repressed and silenced by staying quiet, by settling for everything I didn't want, for saying yes when I meant no. Until that day in the car—my mouth on his cock, his hand on my head, pushing me closer to the woman inside. Except she was no longer woman. She was a child soldier turned warlord, returning for a reckoning to reclaim what I stole.

"A life for a life," she said. "No longer will our body be a coffin; an upright container for quiet deaths. No longer will I conceal bullets and casings to hide your violence. No longer will I swallow your silent screams to save the world from our grief. No longer, woman. No longer, child."

Quiet Deaths
11 March 2022

Poetry died. Not a violent death; the same death as mine—quiet and without a shadow. Here one day, gone the next. And before I knew it, the well of words, that had once overflowed, was empty, bone dry. And like time—slipping away as water slides off skin—poetry and I slipped into the void; her, missing for three years, and me, missing for twenty.

Why are these internal deaths so quiet?

Isn't violence supposed to be loud and uncompromising? A Piercing scream that penetrates the skin of everything. Blood spilling and spurting like monsoon rain. Anguish. Pain. Breaking. Coming undone. Fracturing. Dismantling. Kali. Shiva.

Isn't that what violence is?

Why then, did I die so quietly? Why did I swallow tears, force them down, like a woman forces a cock down her throat, like she swallows to please not herself, but her oppressor, her keeper, her object of desire?

I don't want another quiet death to take place inside

my body. I don't want to hold my tongue, or my breath, or my tears, or my grief, or my hope, or my loneliness, or my longing, or my passion, or my self.

No more quiet deaths.

The next time there is violence, let it be loud and bloody and vengeful. Let me feel the weight of it, pinning me down, fucking me, sparing me nothing.

The next time there is violence, let it break me so unequivocally that my only option is to rebuild.

Drone
15 March 2022 at 12:39

My heart builds an empire
but my head is a drone

above the mist, a single strike

I shouldn't wonder about love
But I wonder, I wonder what to make

of this body of work, so few attempts
yet all of them, failures

Coffins and church bells
ringing and relenting

Loneliness repeating—
a pathetic refrain—

A shadow that can survive
the darkest solstice

I wanted to cure loneliness
18 March 2022

I wanted to cure loneliness
so I drove to the park and took a stranger's cock in my mouth

But the body is merely a vessel
limited in its capacity to house
a grieving heart

And I leave semi-sated
painfully aware that loneliness
is still at home in the passenger seat

Exit Wound
19 March 2022

I wanted to deceive loneliness
so I burrowed into his exit wound

Inside his body, I butterflied my heart
fed it to him, thinking he would choke on wings
before I reached his throat, loneliness was also a boy
with crooked teeth and a dead mother

During the war, love was a weapon I cocked
between my legs, he was a white flag
razing old battlefields, fought and lost
in the year of the tiger, I fell into green hazel

lines, a palm tattooed by voices
heartbeats behind, ahead I'm old enough
to know prayers become wounds, but I prayed
a primal tongue, between prayers I prayed

for spillage, a love to haemorrhage and bleed
into a body, uninhabitable by loneliness

End of my life
20 March 2022 at 13:50

on a park bench
opposite a river ravaged by floods

I spend the day with Ocean

and though he keeps me company
fills my belly with exquisite words
I feel lonelier, and hungrier than the homeless
man asleep on the grass

and though my emotional debris
is rising and breaching,
the high priestess,
whose incantations once converted pain
into pretty poems,
has cut out her tongue to spite her voice

and I sit on a park bench
neither river, nor ocean
contemplating how I will ever make it
to the end of my life without a body
of water, without another drop of rain

Drowning
2 April 2022

I sit here
Alone
in a room full of water
And it's true what they say about drowning
Everyone will see you flounder on the surface
but nobody will see you go under

Oldest dream in the book
21 April 2022 at 14:29

before the skin of time wrinkled it shed
me, a human snake with a heart
as blue as a day old bruise

before the air forgot to breathe it held
my hand, lungs of longing
flowering beneath a sky of birds

before love was a word it was tongue
-tied, tangled in the vocabulary of life
a redacted plot in karma's narrative

before I puzzled over jigsaws
loneliness, my true fault dreaming
the oldest dream in the book

the dream of finding
true love

Vulnerable as a human
22 April 2022 at 10:06

My loneliness is vulnerable;
a human clinging
to fragments of affection

When I kiss and hold you
it's agonising to let go
A beggar, surviving
on the pocket change of time

My body craves more
but my head wins the battle most days
to bring me down, bring me back
to the reality that love is doomed
when Cupid points his arrow at me

Which is why twenty
minutes of you inside
my mouth and body is too painful a curse
to bear when you go
and i wonder if it would be better to stop—

to be lonely all the time
than being torn apart by glimpses of light and stars
unleashed like lightning
every time we touch

My love wears a mask, while I pretend
these fleeting moments are enough
But you must know they are splinters of glass
in my heart
Splinters that will bleed out if I am to keep

pretending
my love for you is not as vulnerable
as a human clinging
to fragments of affection

Eurydice
29 April 2022

In a clearing
I found the king
of the forest
an arrowhead piercing his heart
Caressing his antlers, I kissed his fur
'til tears and blood turned milky

With his last breath
he shed his crown, vowing to follow me
Morpheus in the underworld
the song of Eurydice a step behind

Kingdoms Later
A medicine woman pulls antlers from my chest
It doesn't hurt, but I am devastatingly lonely without them

A dance without music
May 2022

My heart is
confiscated
when yours travels
away
This is not love
Nor is it healthy to lean
only to retreat
a tsunami before it hits
I am human too
in between bouts
Affection, I am lonely
a dance without music
How am I to know if you have stopped breathing?
Or if you've simply stopped breathing for me?

Billie Eilish
May 2022

Billie Eilish is singing about ending up alone and I'm singing along, in my head and out loud, because I am lonely. Not alone, but lonely. Though I have a husband, two children and a dog, I am staggeringly lonely all the time.

What is the root of my loneliness? I'm curious, because while loneliness has always walked beside me, poetry has been my companion; my notepad and pen has kept the melancholy of loneliness at arms length.

Poetry. Perhaps the answer lies on the floor of that restless sea of syllables that has settled and set like volcanic sediment. For three years and counting, Grief has been a boat on the surface, circling and circling.

Anxiety is the desperate search party of one. In between circling, Anxiety jumps into the water and dives to the bottom to scratch and scrape the sediment that has long since solidified.

The only difference between me and Anxiety is that I am no longer panicked. Panic has converted to dread. Dread that the sediment is sealed, and the source of my poetry is dead and buried.

But what is dread if not a relative of fear? And what is fear if not an irrational perspective?

They say that everything must break apart before you can rebuild. I hope this is where I am right now—poised on the verge of great change. Poised on the edge of everything I ever wanted.

Lucid dreaming
May 2022

Like a moth in a blackout
the dark butterfly emerges
wings intact

If these mercurial thoughts turn to birds
they will be caged

So I
shape words into telephone wires
& blades of green grass

Until the birds are only poems
and my loneliness is a lucid
dream

Mockingbird
9 May 2022

How is it that life can change on a dime?
How is it that I can pull butterflies and flowers from a heart that was barren 3 days ago?
How is it that I can find a door behind the moon when it was sealed the last time I travelled?
How is that I have red velvet wings when I had bruised arms a week ago?
How is it that I'm basking in sunshine during monsoon season?
How is it that one lover can turn into a sky of white doves while the other turns into a mockingbird overnight?
Tell me how
How does change take an eternity and an instant simultaneously?

Odin
10 May 2022

Behind the membrane of a dream
two ravens caw

My head is a cocoon
Thoughts and words marinating, dying
in biological soup I wait
on the cusp of metamorphosis
before my skull splits—
a watermelon on concrete

Littered with the bones of quiet deaths
my body is vocal, at the seam
a spinal shift, a fault line
From the fray of black and white
from the softness of cocoon and flight
from the void of day and night

I re-member

Ask Odin and he will tell you the truth:
a raven has more than nine lives

Grandfather
11 May 2022

After the storm, I stopped
alongside a fish pond, I remembered
my grandfather's hands, green
his inventions mocked,
outlandish, Funny
how recycled spirits arrive
too early
instead of
fashionably late
I wonder if he also saw the future
I wonder if he knew my suffering
would be translated into books

Lepidopterist
20 May 2022

I tell myself that poetry has died
but I'm a liar

The poems still come
Only now I daren't
scatter them to the wind

Now, I pin them down,
like a lepidopterist pins butterflies
inside glass frames

Egypt
8 June 2022

Like an old testament plague, I am Egypt

cursed by my own hand, I have darkened the sky
excommunicated sunshine from my fingers

the creative womb, wide as the Nile
suspended in dead sea salt
has shrivelled,

drought-stricken, I swarm,
a locust devouring every tree
of knowledge, every branch
of thought, every leaf
of experience, every seed
of observation, Poetry

is, has become, a memory
vivid, fading, unreliable

and though a thousand blank pages of new testament
wait, my pen is neither fluid nor fluent

The Exodus is complete

1326:
10 June 2022

As I type my last goodbye
Halsey sings about dying for love and burying bodies

And I should shed a tear
for this loss is real
and the seeds of grief beneath my skin are sprouting
into roses laced with thorns

And although their blossoms prick
and pierce, leaving a trail of blood droplets

the pain of letting you go is less acute
than the pain of keeping you

Like your hands at my throat before orgasm
you are letting go when you should be squeezing
because your threshold between fear and love is paper
thin—
so easily breached

And so I will water these roses every day now
Each day I will welcome thorns,
welcome blood shedding,
welcome bloodletting.

Like a modern day witch, who is wise
to the poison garden that could have grown,
I will not stay a minute longer
with a lover who is afraid of love.

Europa
5 July 2022

What am i to do with this rose
rooted in my spine, blooming
like one of Jupiter's moons—
Europa, Io, Callisto, Ganymede

Am I to yank it?
Am i to bleed out?

Why can't I keep it?
Why can't it grow unchecked?

And If I am to yank it
If i am to bleed out
Then why not swallow petals and thorns
as a last resort?
Why not water them
with tears and longing
So maybe, just maybe,
my rose will grow back
    like a bird released
    but possessing no desire
    to fly away

If only you knew the depth
If only i could tell

If only
If only
I didn't always trap and keep my heart this way

Europa's vast ocean, sealed
beneath an icy crust

Hotel
17 July 2022

Inside the hotel, black and white photographs draw me toward bone white walls. On sighting a stag's crown between winter branches, the ghost behind my ribs stirs.

Thoughts travel to the house on the river where a medicine woman pulled a trophy from my chest—certain I would be better for it. But all I have felt since is a crushing sense of loss. As if the woman had severed a spiritual limb from the core of my being. As if the stag had stabbed me in the chest during mating season.

I dream of those antlers night after night, seeking out Hades each time I'm under. Devil or Faust—I do not care. Without those antlers I am lost, incomplete. The king of the forest once lived inside me. Now, his death is a mirror and I am the hunter who fired the fatal shot.

Freezing Point
24 July 2022

Light streams through a cell window
though it is overcast outside
hope is sometimes faint

Silence is an element
below freezing point i burrow
deep inside winter to hear

muted voices, soon to be
extinguished inside
a head full of fire

Love reimagined
26 July 2022 at 13:12

A bird falls
free of its wings, my heart floats

a feather on the open road, love is
an infinite journey, will you walk with me

when I travel, with fear and faith
tucked inside your pockets, will you trust me

when I fly away, when I chase ghosts
haunt me, will you be there

when love is a lesson, fear and ego
are cacophonous, will you listen

when I sing, songs from a cage
sound sweeter, will you flock

flightless, birds of a feather
stick together, could you love

a bird who falls
free of its wings

I wanted to murder loneliness
11 August 2022

I wanted to murder loneliness, so I drove to a graveyard and started digging. But death requires a body, and loneliness is a layer of skin.

Loneliness is the ugly brown birthmark that my mother said would grow bigger each birthday. And, while she was wrong about the birthmark, her theory held water. Loneliness has grown bigger and uglier - a darker stain every year.

The closer I get to the boundary of mortality, loneliness grows godlike in its omnipotent power. And each year I worship it more reverently and fearfully. *Please don't condemn me for eternity*, I say. *I am worthy of love. I will do anything*, I beg. *Have mercy on me*, I pray.

I'm old enough to know that prayers go unanswered - especially those uttered in desperation and need. So perhaps my real flaw is hope. I need hope more than faith, more than proof, more than answers. To live without hope is to die piecemeal.

Funny thing, though, I'm already dying piecemeal.

With loathing's tongue in my mouth and fear's fingers at my throat, I am already dying. I have already dug my grave.

Which makes this thing called hope, false. But I am also king and queen of denial. Aren't I? Like Hannibal Lecter in his windowless cell, I have engineered a suspension bridge between the monolith of my reality and the blue yonder of my mind. And there, in that mythical wonderland, is a life worth dying for, instead of this death I am living for.

But false hope is better than no hope when all is said and done, so I continue to build an internal world of cards - a flimsy stack that gets taller each year. And each year I grow more diligent in my mastery over balancing that stack. For the worst thing in the world would be a toppling. A toppling for which there may be no comeback. For a life's work is quite something - dramatic and deep - an ocean, an abyss - the depth and breadth of which is unimaginable.

And I ask myself: What if your world toppled? What would you do? Where would you possibly begin to find that needle of hope in a haystack?

And though it is rhetorical, I hear an unequivocal voice from the muffled depths:

It has toppled, you loser.

*Hope was the body, and
loneliness is her pathetic ghost.*

Ode to becoming a love letter
22 September 2022

Lilac blooms
in provincial woods of my mind
between trees of old me
magic appears like shooting stars

I glimpse the dusty, old Empress,
centuries of past lives lining
the bookshelves of her soul

Bring a light with you, she says
The sky is a dark rose
who weeps when you walk and hide
in the shadows

Foreign ghosts strum my heart strings
winter gives way to spring
Through a labyrinth of flowers
we converse among the ruins
There is no place like home

One hundred and twenty seven
thoughts
My mood is sentimental
A silver lining peeks around the corner
with raindrops on its nose

September has flown
away and come back to nest
again, my heart is a bowl of feathers
My feet are free to dance
in another land, where hope glimmers

Nestled in wildflower stalks
I lie in the grass and gaze
at the sky
Why is not a question to wield anymore

My fingers are poised, itching even
to begin writing seventy four
pages of happiness
An ode to becoming a love letter

A Happy Man
23 September 2022

From this place of uncertainty
I can dig
a grave to bury the past, plant
ghosts underground
Knowing crocuses will rise
Don't try to explain
why
on this September morn
I dream of fireflies and daffodils
while dancing to Jazz in a basement kitchen
Love may take a while—
negatives in a dark room
Like the Eiffel tower at night, I am the colour
of tangled flames
knowing full well that his only need
is to die
a happy man

A blossom of hope
23 September 2022

On rainy days I freefall
A blossom of hope growing pale
between dreams yet to shine

The journey of becoming
is an epilogue of longing
horizontal lines that never meet

Will I find solace from endurance
or is peace a reflection
wide awake at daybreak

Some days I am
the embodiment of tangerine
memories floating on land
A dissolution of matter
Searching for a song of hope

Gold thread
24 September 2022

Could I be stitched
inside black and white reality
when I could tug
on a dream's gold thread?

To tease and coax an unformed thought
is to tipple into a lake of honey
So I float
inside a song

At night the wind shares
secrets about where it's been
I do not want to leave myself behind again
but my body parts are heavier than moon rock

To run on water is to conquer
demons
but I am still
drowning, still treading, still swimming

Ghostwriter

30 September 2022

Dear Bianca,

I'm watching you as you sit in a lonely cafe, trying to write something, anything.

And though I am a ghost— less tangible than smoke—I can still feel the pain in your gut as if it is my own.

I can feel the lump in your throat, applauding, as you beg the tears to remain seated. I can hear your thoughts as if they were children yelling in my ears. Desperation, anger, frustration, and the never ending echo of why?

Why? That rock you throw into the abyss, expecting to hear a splash. But the abyss is shallow when compared to your greatest fear.

The fear that your gift is dead and buried. And all that remains is its ghost—a phantom poet who is stalking and haunting you from a wasteland of words.

Yours,
Ghostwriter

Ripening
1 October 2022 at 14:35

Below a ripening moon
a vermilion moth stirs
its folded wings

I hear humming, feel vibrations in my belly
Tangled emotions catch
in my throat, a bumble bee looms large

The tea-stained cloth in my hand
falls
a yellowed piano key
sustained————it is slow motion
a window of déjà-vu

Time is tangible—a person standing opposite me
i dig inside my head and heart
questions that only time can answer
For i have grown older of late—
with unrivalled speed
And i don't want to die without knowing
why i am here

Outside,
the crimson moth stirs and flies
toward the moon, i blink,

a nanosecond—

Time is a child
with a penny
the moment is spent

i ponder that for a while
Ponder how fleeting and fragile
we are when we stop, when we slow down
long enough to feel
    the tightness in our gut, to hear
        the little voice, to witness
            our shadows decaying as our mortal timeline
                darkens on the horizon

When will I stop?
When will anything ever be enough?

Koru
11 October 2022 at 12:26

I wish i could comfort you
with elegant thoughts
But no lie could suspend these wild birds
that twist mid flight in my head

Koru—a silver fern crowning
Like a surprise, I unfurl
Another painful death, or is it forty eight rebirths

Wrists and ankles bound
androgynous shame
If my hips could speak
Her voice would be fluid
and certain
My antithesis, surely

I / My / Me
restless
a chaotic dragon
perpetually hungry for a master
whose shadow shrinks against mine
If only i could remove the scales, see
the sweet truth of my innocent power
Instead, I am mired in the trenches of a treasonous
mind

No ceasefire in sight

A listless philosophy is dangerous
for a stranger like me
Living by the sword of absurdity and nihilism
day in and out, while harbouring a medicine
woman inside my chest

Egg Shells
16 October 2022

Dreams I have planted
but weeds grow taller and thicker

Each year
I shrink, a violet raindrop on eggshells

The ghosts welcome me again
It's been a minute since we communed and co-existed

What am I to do without my gift
The piano weeps while I sleepwalk

Fit for a queen's throne
yet bloodied by a crown of thorns
Why has this madness made its home inside me

Striving for stars that could be optical illusions
Unless I look into the mirror, the moon
is the only dragon I see

Oh, and when longing strikes
twilight, when it ticks past midnight

my ribs are caged birds
and I am an inkwell of craving

Medusa
17 October 2022 at 10:17

I have muted my voice and colours for camouflage sake
But death does not become a wild seed

I have buried antlers deeper than bone
Hidden feminine virility for fear of becoming
Medusa in Athena's temple
destined to be struck down
A starling beneath the falcon's talon
The stag caught in the rifle's sight

But now
an inner moon bursts into a ball of light
stars bleed from my veins
My heart's compass is back on course
The magnet of mayhem removed

It has been eons
since I've seen the eyes of my soul
i will not be blinded again by the spear of an ego whose
only prey is limitation and fear-based pursuits

I will fight you, my passenger
I am potent, i am virile
Stand down, step away, or be crushed by my hooves
I will bow no longer to your skewed wisdom, your

inherent lies
I have seen your face, i have excavated the bones of
your disfigured truth
and i am not the haggard crone you painted me to be

We will fight to the death, you and I
and i will win
for I am queen, i am king
on the throne of breakthroughs

Bow or be gone
The forest will absolve you on your way out

Love Poem
22 October 2022 at 17:41

When night falls beneath our skin
we will find love
Behind shadows and inside the night bird's
song of surrender
Find love we will, night after night,
until we're ready to let go
Until we're ready to dream alone
Until then, we will love
with every breath

Though rain sometimes falls
from our eyes the moon sleeps
inside, a ribcage of longing
a flower garden for a heart
more fertile than the love planted
within its walls

there are seeds, a sprinkling of hope
We kiss time on the forehead
build a staircase behind our spines
To tarry or to leave
We tuck these thoughts beneath silk pillowcases,
ask the stars to gather—
a constellation to outlast time

Love could be rose
or love could be a thorn
If we never let go, my love
if we never let go

Peony Pavilion
19 November 2022

We survived stillness,
stars,
stürm and drang
from behind dark wood partitions
He, a corridor of floor and paper
Me, a match and a flame
a bowing woman, meandering
toward the peony pavilion

In a jade tea hall I fell
asleep. dreamed
inside rooms of yellow gold
a firebird at the edge of the sun, my cheeks alight
scissors could not untangle his grief
so I opened my heart like a window
waiting for the Japanese lilac to blossom

In an emerald forest I woke
on a bed of red leaves, a woman with three hearts
inside her ribcage, a kingdom of flowers
growing at time lapse
burgeoning and morphing
into trees too beautiful
to fell

Mudita
20 November 2022

I know who lives behind his smile
and that his heart is a white
bird with blood-specked feathers

I know that we have survived
between parallel grooves of an ancient city
walking up stone stairways each day
to face the adjudicator of a pounding heart

I know that we have crossed
origami oceans and concrete waves
between sips
of carnation tea

And I know
Mudita
is the hardest virtue to master

Linguist
20 November 2022

I have studied love
a linguist licking roots
of a semantic memory
Partial, I am
always have been
to etymological boulders, to thunderous mythology
It was always the fairytales
that were untethered,
floating,
one-dimensional speech bubbles

I have read bastardised versions
I have explored the truth—
and I have graduated knowing
that love is alive
Like a soul, it has a life of its own
love breathes its own breath—
the body cannot contain it

I have written about love
the lines will never stop
exploring
the mercurial woman
who Blossoms and wilts
like a human flower

Whose theories cannot be melted
like crucible steel
Whose heart is wilder
than the skeleton coast

Thief
4 December 2022

Life has stretched
a mark that can't be smoothed
with coconut oil or tangerine
In the shadow of the lighthouse
at the cliff edge, loneliness no longer chimes on the hour
It is not the end, it is never the end

For years I saw a bird without wings
staring back at me
And ever since, I've been kneeling on the ocean floor
watching hurricanes from a blue hole
willing time to drag or crush me
once and for all

But time was a smoke ring
in Prévert's Breakfast—
indifferent to my heartache
"inviolate darkness"
always for the first time

Now, as years turn to epiphanies
and thoughts of death retreat
I see old friends
loneliness and failure refracting

brilliant shards of a mirror ravaged by superstition
and I see my hour upon the stage—a mind impenetrable
by light

but now an alchemist turning
what if into when
a field of stars beneath my feet
a galaxy of time in my palms
a dazzling thief, always
on the verge
of breakthrough

Notes and Acknowledgements

1. Many thanks to Richard Gibney for writing a sterling and thoughtful introduction.

2. Thanks to the Editor of Shot Glass Journal Issue #31 for publishing the poem TATTOOIST

3. TEMPO RUBATO
Tempo rubato is an Italian musical phrase that literally means "stolen time". It refers to intuitive shifting that makes music sound expressive and natural. Nineteenth century composer-pianist Frédéric Chopin is often mentioned in the context of rubato.

4. ROME
Sulpicia (1) is thought to have lived during the reign of Emperor Augustus, and is the only female poet from Ancient Rome whose poetry has survived. Sulpicia's six love elegies, published by Tibullus in Corpus Tibullianum, record her love affair with a young man whom she calls 'Cerinthus' (a Greek pseudonym). The word Cērinthus is Latin, meaning bee-bread or pollen, and, by extension, the food of bees.

Over the centuries, scholars have contested Sulpicia's authorship and credibility, arguing on one hand that the patriarchal system would have precluded a woman from participating in what was a highly educated man's domain, and on the other hand asserting that a woman was incapable of writing anything of literary worth, least of all poems. However, it is now widely accepted that Sepulcia, the daughter of upper class parents connected to Augustus's inner circle, would have been highly educated. Further connections have been drawn between Sulpicia's uncle, Marcus Valerius Messalla Corvinus (a patron of literature) and Tibullus, who was a prominent member of Messalla's Literary Circle, which would explain how Sulpicia's poems were published in Tibullus's book.

Sources:
Love, Sex and Marriage in Ancient Rome
https://www.worldhistory.org/article/1592/love-sex--marriage-in-ancient-rome/

Sulpicia (1) - Oxford Classical Dictionary
https://oxfordre.com/classics/display/10.1093/acrefore/9780199381135.001.0001/acrefore-9780199381135-e-6126;jsessionid=178CF127872B2694496180B0178BDA27

Sulpicia (1) - Women in Antiquity
https://womeninantiquity.wordpress.com/2017/03/26/sulpicia-i/

Love Has Finally Arrived - My Translation of Sulpicia (1)
https://thebookbindersdaughter.com/2017/08/04/love-has-finally-arrived-my-translation-of-sulpicia/

Albius Tibullus - Britannica
https://www.britannica.com/biography/Albius-Tibullus

Marcus Valerius Messalla Corvinus - Britannica
https://www.britannica.com/biography/Marcus-Valerius-Messalla-Corvinus

Cerinthus
https://www.latin-is-simple.com/en/vocabulary/noun/4881/

The Significance of the Name Cerinthus in the Poems of Sulpicia
https://www.jstor.org/stable/283989
Roessel, David. "The Significance of the Name Cerinthus in the Poems of Sulpicia." Transactions of the American Philological Association (1974-) 120 (1990): 243–50. https://doi.org/10.2307/283989.

5. EURYDICE
Eurydice was a nymph in Greek mythology who was

married to Orpheus, a legendary musician and poet. One day, while walking in the forest, Aristaeus pursued Eurydice, who tried to evade him by running away. She was bitten by a snake and died. Orpheus was so devastated that he made a deal with Hades, the god of the underworld. Orpheus was to walk ahead of Eurydice and not look back until they both reached the surface. However, when nearing daylight, Orpheus wondered if Hades was tricking him and he turned back, only to see Eurydice disappear back into the underworld.
Source: https://www.greekmythology.com/Myths/Mortals/Eurydice/eurydice.html

6. EUROPA

Jupiter has 80 moons, but the 4 largest are called Lo, Europa, Ganymede and Callista. Each of these moons are distinctive worlds. While Jupiter cannot support life as we know it, some of these moons have oceans beneath their crusts that might support life.
Source: Nasa

7. A HAPPY MAN

According to Greek legend the crocus plant is named after Krokus, a mortal youth who died of unrequited love for the shepherdess Smilax. After his death, the gods turned him into a crocus plant. Another version states that when Krokus died, three tears fell into the flower and became its three stigma.

Source: https://en.m.wikipedia.org/wiki/Crocus

Fireflies are said to flash their light in specific patterns in order to attract the perfect mate.
Source: https://www.wellandgood.com/firefly-meaning/amp/

8. KORU
The Koru is a spiral shape based on the unfurling silver fern frond. It is a common symbol of creation in Māori art.

9. MEDUSA
Medusa - an evil woman with snakes for hair who turned men to stone with one look; or a beautiful young woman who was raped by Poseidon, punished by Athena and beheaded by Perseus?

How we frame a story changes the meaning.

10. MUDITĀ
Muditā is a sanskrit word meaning sympathetic or vicarious joy that comes from delighting in other people's wellbeing. The English equivalent is compersion. To practice compersion is to view an individual as autonomous and celebrate their own unique path to fulfillment.

11. PEONY PAVILION
Stürm and drang is German for "storm and stress". It was also a proto-Romantic movement in German literature and music, during the 18th Century, that gave free expression to individual subjectivity and extremes of emotion.

The Peony Pavilion is a romantic tragicomedy play written by dramatist Tang Xianzu in 1598.

12. LINGUIST
In ancient times steel and iron were impossible to melt because temperatures were not high enough. Crucible steel, made with cast iron, had a higher carbon content and lower melting point.

13. THIEF
"inviolate darkness" / always for the first time—is from André Breton's poem Toujour la première fois.

A blue hole is a marine cavern or sinkhole in which sediment accumulates at the bottom. Like a tree ring grows each year, layers of sediment build up in blue holes, and these layers are used by paleotempestologists (scientists who study historical tropical cyclone activity) to count how many hurricanes have passed through.
Source: Smithsonianmag.com

About the Author

Bianca Bowers is an immigrant, best-selling poetry author, novelist and award-winning poetry editor. She holds a BA in English and Film/TV/Media Studies and has authored several books through her imprints Paperfields Press and Auteur Books.

She is known for her deeply personal writing style that seamlessly weaves cultural and literary references into work that is informed by life experience and inspired by love, relationships, personal evolution, and the human condition.

Bianca's first poems were published in 1999, in the esteemed New Zealand poetry anthology, Tongue in your Ear. Since then, Bianca's poems have appeared in various print anthologies, online journals and a trailer for a short film.

THIEF is Bianca's sixth poetry collection. Her second novel, THE WINEMAKER'S WIFE, is due in 2023.

You can find her at:
www.biancabowers.com
www.instagram.com/BiancaBowers_Author
https://amazon.com/author/biancabowers
https://www.goodreads.com/BiancaBowersAuthor

A Note From the Author

Dear Reader,

Thank you for supporting my work.

To help it reach a wider audience, please consider rating it and/or writing a review on Amazon, Goodreads, or the online shop you purchased it from.

Reviews are crucial due to algorithms and they needn't be long or complex. It's essentially a thumbs up to other readers that it's worth their time.

Alternatively, you can post a shopping link with an excerpt from your favourite poem on your chosen social media platform and share it with your followers and friends.

Thank you,

Bianca xo

<u>Review Links:</u>
https://amazon.com/author/biancabowers
https://www.goodreads.com/BiancaBowersAuthor

Other books by Bianca Bowers

CAPE OF STORMS (AUTEUR BOOKS, 2019)

When eight year old Rosalinde collides with apartheid in the summer of 1982, her entire belief system is thrown into chaos and the infrastructure of her world begins to decay.

Set over two decades, Rosalinde's tumultuous story moves between atmospheric locations like the Skeleton Coast, Karoo, Cape Point, and KwaMashu, and hosts an array of vivid characters, including Mohini, her mystical Hindu maid, the charismatic Paris and his radical cousin Maleven; Mark, the ex-soldier; and Rosalinde's two uncles — the wealthy, but austere Uncle Jericho, and the predatory, racist Uncle Léon.

While navigating personal injustice, family sagas, romance, and political unrest, Rosalinde's coming-of-age parallels the years of apartheid's climactic end, against an increasingly violent backdrop, and she learns that the human condition of her motherland is far more complex than she ever imagined.

REVIEWS

"A gripping and unforgettable account of one of humanity's great failures, told with sensitivity and eloquence from a uniquely powerful perspective."
~ Self-Publishing Review

"Bowers pulls no punches in the narrative. Her first-hand knowledge lends authenticity to the experiences of the powerful and the powerless in an environment both beautiful and brutal."
~ J.P. McLean, Author of The Gift Legacy

"I cannot praise this book enough. I would give it more than 5 stars if I could. It moved me in a great way – from utter hopelessness to high triumphs. I cannot recommend it enough. Read it! Read it with an open heart and prepare to be whisked away on a beautiful, terrifying journey."
~ Laura Maybrooke, Author of Dulcea's Rebellion Trilogy

BUTTERFLY VOYAGE (PAPERFIELDS PRESS, 2018)

 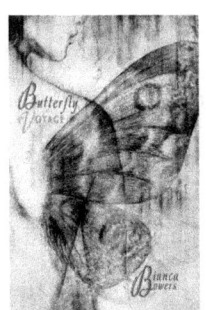

Butterfly Voyage is a shamanic journey that unfurls through a poetic conversation between a spirit mother, Leda, and her daughter, Butterfly...

> *I am the mother / who always loved you*
> *Feathers for arms / Tattoos for skin*
> *I was the mother / she was the sin*

Shape shifting into various spirit animals — black dragon, crocodile, raven — Leda slowly but surely guides Butterfly away from her well of self-loathing and toward self-love by healing old emotional wounds, rewriting disempowering narratives, and rediscovering the magic of authenticity.

> *"Those wings that look like ribs / are real*
> *The pain is not mistaken, Butterfly"*

REVIEWS

"Beautiful, a work of art! This book stoked the flames in my heart and spoke to my restlessness. While it was introduced to me as poetry, I place it in line with the Seth books, Ram Dass, or Emmanuel Book 1."

~ Amazon USA

"It is a beautiful book that speaks of life lessons, easy, hard, far reaching, evolving, and permanent. It's a book about life and living it, no matter the gender, age, or baggage you may have, for you are human, you are beautiful, and you can fly."

~ J.D. Estrada, Author

This is truly a magnificent poetry collection full of magic, discovery and wonder. The words take you away to different realms-landscapes of hazy dreams and ancient dragons. Hidden messages echo and are revealed throughout her life as she unravels herself through a healing shamanic journey. This is a call to rediscover your true authentic self and shake off the negativity, the shackles that held us throughout our lifetimes. There is a resilience in spirit that helps us rise out of self destruction and the helplessness of victimhood. This is an amazing piece of work and one of my all time favorite poetry books!!

~ Michael C. Anderson, Poetry Author

LOVE IS A SONG SHE SANG FROM A CAGE (PAPERFIELDS PRESS, 2016)

In her third book of poetry, Bianca Bowers explores the complexities of love and challenges the convention of monogamy.

"I think of Anthony and Cleopatra...epic, fated, tragic lovers that drank from love's cup but once. Only, I am no Cleopatra. I am Juliette, with her teenage desire; ambivalent about poison and war."

Ruminating the one-love-fits-all theory, and toying with the concept of polyamory, the poetic voice travels from a starting point in which forbidden love poses a dilemma worthy of a Shakespearean-tragedy to a more indignant ending in which "our brains are slaveowners and love was never meant to be imprisoned."

REVIEWS

This collection of poems by Bianca Bowers is a journey towards freedom. These poems are strong, evocative and powerfully written. Read individually or through as a story in it's own right, Love Is A Song... stirs a powerful song that is worth singing it's way down from the bookshelf again and again.
~ Amazon USA

"Bianca's imagery is sophisticated, considered and beautiful."
~ Amazon UK

"Bianca's words are fulcrums upon which she balances emotions."
~ Amazon CA

PASSAGE (PAPERFIELDS PRESS, 2015)

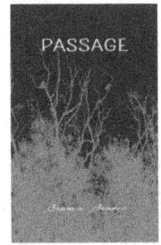 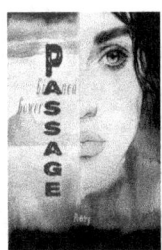

"My feet were fused with a 7-lane highway. My spine, dismantled; a map of bones with no instruction."

In her second book of poetry, Bianca Bowers deconstructs and redefines her identity beyond marriage and motherhood while searching for an unattainable sense of belonging as an Australian immigrant.

With a mix of surreal poems and poetry firmly grounded in reality, Bowers shifts effortlessly between consciousness and sleep, reality and dreams, as she seeks to find passage in a restless landscape.

"When I find my voice / it muzzles the lark's chorus... My roots shrivel below the heath / but harebells bloom from my fingertips."

REVIEWS

"Bianca seems to hover above her own conversation as if she herself is observing from the outside in."
~ Amazon USA

"Bianca has a beautiful way of capturing intense feelings and articulating them in a very poignant way that cuts to the bone and pierces the heart."
~ Amazon AU

DEATH AND LIFE (PAPERFIELDS PRESS, 2014)

"Death is the great disruptor. It thrusts us opposite life's mirror, invites our truthful exploration, and reveals the naked truth from which rebirth is possible and we are free to reinvent ourselves anew."

Death and Life is the first poetry book by Bianca Bowers, and includes poems and essays written between 1987 and 2013.

Dedicated to those who struggle in their youth, and autobiographical in nature, she invites you to journey through various psychological, emotional, and spiritual experiences to discover why death is not isolated to physical loss, but extends to figurative deaths that arise from larger themes such as patriarchy, abuse, depression, love, exile, belonging, and identity.

*"Change
blows through the branches of our existence
and fortifies the roots on which we stand."*

REVIEWS

"As I delved into this I was taken by surprise at the myriad of emotions that I experienced. I was deeply saddened, I smiled so broadly that it lit a room, I laughed and I cried, memories of my own so long lost were rekindled."
~ Amazon USA

"It's like reading a refined journal that you wrote long ago — one that touches you to the core and captures everything you ever thought you knew of the mystery of life and death and love."
~ Amazon USA

"Bowers shares her journey with such honesty that one cannot help but be in the moment with her. I suffered her loss, heartbreak and anguish and was rewarded with liberation, self-reflection and love."
~ Amazon USA

"Death and Life takes the reader on a journey of true experience by someone that has obviously travelled the tracks from darkness through to the light, and beyond. Amazing work by an incredibly talented poet."
~ Amazon USA

PRESSED FLOWERS (PAPERFIELDS PRESS, 2018)

*"We pick flowers, knowing they will die.
We press flowers, hoping they will survive."*

Reading a poem is not so different to picking a flower. Like flowers, there are some poems we want to press between the pages of a book.

This book contains eighty six of my most popular poems from my first three books: Death and Life (2014), Passage (2015), and Love Is A Song She Sang From A Cage (2016).

EDITORIAL REVIEWS

Like many of the finest scribes, such as continental Irishmen Beckett and Joyce, Bianca Bowers is an exile. A poet and author originally from South Africa, now living in Australia, she often writes about rootlessness and place, and searches for a definition – or redefines the idea of – "home" in a variety of ways.

Bowers' poems frequently have a power, whether through the force of the language to which she's clearly entitled given her eloquence, through a compulsion to claim the aforementioned space, or to articulate themes such as motherhood and aspects of the feminine.

There is a very creative exploitation of language throughout this collection. What we can assume to be a road surface, hot underfoot, is described as "solar-powered tar"; in the same poem, a "secret sin" is apparently sent out as a bottled message into the sea in an act of catharsis. In this and other work, Bowers has a remarkable capacity to surprise.

There are images and ideas throughout Bowers' work to inspire further thoughts and ideas, concepts and themes that leave this reader both contemplative and envious in an "I wish I'd thought of that" way.

~ Richard Gibney

www.ingramcontent.com/pod-product-compliance
Lightning Source LLC
Chambersburg PA
CBHW050319010526
44107CB00055B/2316